Palasandra

Book One of the Kiger Collection

Mark Friedrich

ISBN 979-8-89112-731-9 (Paperback)
ISBN 979-8-89112-732-6 (Digital)

Covenant Books
11661 Hwy 707
Murrells Inlet, SC 29576
www.covenantbooks.com

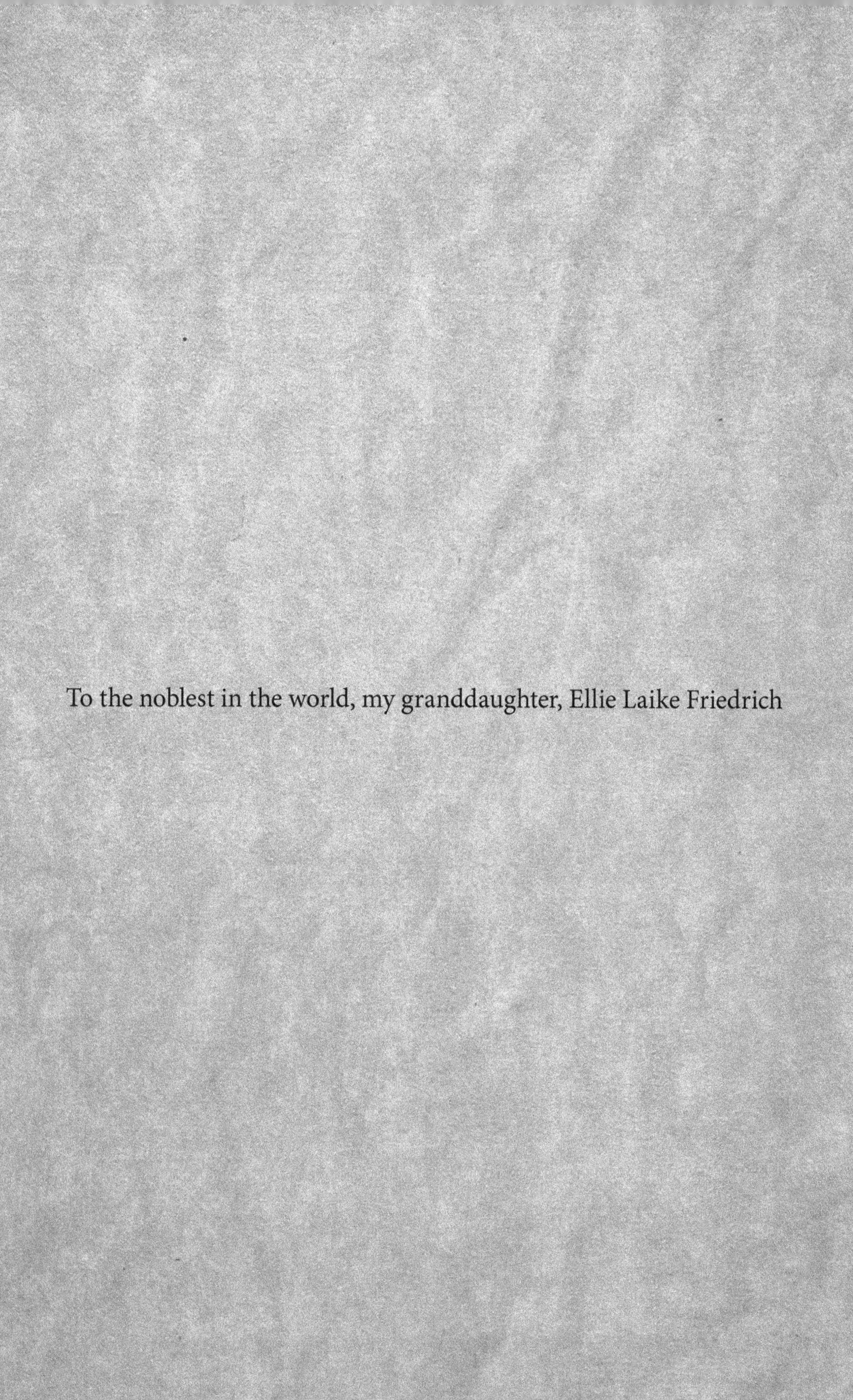

To the noblest in the world, my granddaughter, Ellie Laike Friedrich

Acknowledgment

I want to remember three people who had a profound influence on my life. First, my great-uncle, Harry Friedrich, who was a horse trainer and trader, I loved walking to his house on Saturdays so I could go to the horse sale with him. Watching him work and listening to his stories inspired and enriched my life tremendously. Second, my great-aunt, Johanna Parr, and my grandmother, Marie Metcalfe, who taught me the golden rules of life, they always encouraged me to go after what life offers and to get back up when life knocks me down. These strong women showed me that I could be whatever I wanted to be, and for that, I never wanted to let them down. I thank them for their love and encouragement when I was young.

I'd also like to mention the following people who helped make this book possible:

Michael Slaughter

Kelly Gibson

Rick Littleton

Josh Warburton

Tom Whalen, Colleen Kimball, Stacey Vohland, and Annah Sparks of Technicraft

Mark Marcek with In Print Graphics Inc.

Susan Carson, illustrator

My family and all the horse friends I've made along the way.

Finally, thanks be to God for saving this cowboy's soul.

The noblest question in the world is what good may I do in it.

(Benjamin Franklin)

Preface

Much has been written about the wild horses of North America, but very little is known about a breed of horses called the Kiger mustang. In 1977, a small band of Spanish horses was discovered in the high deserts of Oregon. Much like the wild horses from thousands of years ago, the entire herd had markings called the dun factor—primitive coloration with zebra-striped legs and a dorsal stripe down the back. Where did they come from? How did they get there? We may never know the actual story. Some facts are known, but the rest is for guessing and dreaming. Only our imagination can fill in the missing events. This is the story of Palasandra and how she and her herd may have lived before they were rediscovered.

I am Palasandra, the matriarch of the majestic Kiger mustang breed. My ancestors came to the Americas with the Spanish conquistadors over five hundred years ago. Their names may be forgotten, but their spirit lives on through me and my offspring.

We came from the ancient ones. They were a breed of horse that lived on the plains of Andalusia, Spain. We came from superior breeding lines. My family came from the royal stables of King Ferdinand and Queen Isabella.

We voyaged across the great ocean in a mighty sailing vessel to serve the conquering explorer, Francisco Coronado, in his search for the lost city of gold. Cibola! We were explorers and warhorses!

My story is true. It begins as we escaped from the Spaniards and flourished on the western plains of the new world. We were new to its perils.

The grass and flowers remembered us from prehistoric times. The ancient herds grazed here too! The great Creator made us free to be a proud, majestic horse with a will and spirit to survive.

We ran wild and free and prospered on every range available to us. We lived by the law of nature. Only the strong survived. Millions of horses lived and passed through life's perilous journey in this new land.

My family's herd flourished and migrated further west into the great wonders of a wild new world. We lived free for hundreds of years with no human master.

$\mathscr{T}$he centuries washed by, and we grew into a strong, vibrant part of the natural world. We took our rightful place among the many strange creatures that became our friends and our enemies.

We were counted in the millions. We became as many as the stars in the heavens above us.

ome of us became partners with the native Shoshoni Indian cultures; they had never seen a horse. They named us Patabeya Sadee, which translates to elk dogs, big and swift like an elk and smart like a dog! Through their stories, a remembrance song was sung for us.

We served them well and they respected us. They believed we were gifts of powerful medicine from the great Creator.

When the Europeans came to settle the west, many of us were captured and destroyed. They wanted the land we shared. We were enslaved and served them.

They mixed our blood with the blood of their horses. We fought on both sides of the great battles between the native Indians and the white Europeans. Once again, we became brave war horses.

After the great wars, our pure blood was diminished, and the great herds were lost. My family fled and disappeared into the rugged high mountain deserts in a land called Oregon, where no man would go.

A few of my royal family were still alive and free. My great mother and father and a small herd of relatives found a sanctuary in the lofty, isolated mountains.

*I*solated and separated, we banded together and survived the extreme elements. The conditions were harsh. The weather, the terrain, the wolves, and the cougars were treacherous. The food was scarce. We searched until we found pastures of lush grass and fresh water. We adapted to the conditions.

We became even stronger and went back to our primitive, natural ways. Through hope, faith, and a determination to survive, we continued in the struggle to keep our herds alive. The great Creator took care of us.

My great mother and great father were the last of our royal family. From a family of a few horses, they started over. My mother ruled the herd. They began once more to continue our legacy.

I was born and grew up strong in our hidden mountain sanctuary. When my time came, I ascended to take my place as the lead mare of my herd.

$\mathcal{M}$esteno arose from the other royal herd and became my partner and stallion. Together we assembled our family. We bore many foals together.

He fought for us. He protected us. He loved us. He was the new king of our race. Once again, we were the strong, wild, and free mustang roaming the western plains.

My reign was long, prosperous, and full of horse memories. I ruled and led my herd with Mesteno. He was grander than all of the stallions before him. He was our peaceful ruler. I loved him and he loved me! We shared our new secret home. We bonded together to rebuild our herd in the high desert mountains.

I became the great mother of our breed. My children became the Kiger mustang. We had overcome the hardships and survived to build a new history for the wild Spanish horse of America. We were kings and queens of all the wild horses.

Our story is never-ending. My descendants have their own tales to tell. They have a place in this world. You can join us. I, Palasandra, and Mesteno are running free with the ancient ones now. Fear not, for we live in the hearts and spirits of the sons and daughters in a new generation of wild mustang. I am Palasandra. My spirit lives on forever.

Palasandra and Mesteno were real wild horses that lived in a mountainous area called Beatty's Butte, Oregon. They lived free until 1977 when a Bureau of Land Management agent discovered them. Palasandra and Mesteno's herd was rounded up. They were removed from their home and relocated to a region called Kiger Gorge. The government agency evaluated and tested them for Spanish DNA. They were found to be as pure as a breed can be. They matched up so closely with Spanish Andalusian's and Spain's Sorria horses that the agency decided to observe and save them as one of the last true representatives of horses the conquistadors had brought to the Americas.

How Palasandra, Mesteno, and their ancestors survived and developed for so long without being discovered and without any mixed blood influencing the herd is a mystery. The herd was split up for management purposes and was allowed to breed freely. The two herds were called the Riddle Mountain herd and the Kiger Gorge herd. Palasandra and Mesteno lived the rest of their lives at Kiger Gorge. About every four years, they were gathered up, and the babies and some young horses were auctioned off to the public.

Palasandra and Mesteno along with a few mares were turned loose after each round up. Palasandra and Mesteno's family became the largest herd on Kiger Gorge. They became very elusive and were difficult to track and find. On their last round-up, Mesteno was injured. He was returned to the wild along with Palasandra and the remaining mares and was never rounded up again. Mesteno overcame his injury but was growing old. He could no longer defend the herd from interloper stallions. Palasandra did it for him, and she was loyal to her stallion. She protected Mesteno and the herd. He stayed with Palasandra until the end. His reign was thirty years. Mesteno was last seen at the herd's watering hole taking a drink. He then disappeared. Palasandra kept the herd together and tenaciously fought off other stallions. She was always the lead mare of her family herd.

Palasandra was last seen leading her band of mares out of Kiger Gorge and headed home.

Mark Friedrich lives and works at Muddy Creek Farms in Central Florida. He is an accomplished horse rancher and master builder. His other interests are photography and art and now endeavors to write about the history and lives of Muddy Creek Kiger horses. Many of the ranch's horses are now in Europe and Canada, and others are living in various ranches in the United States.

It was from the very stables of Muddy Creek Farms that Mark was inspired to write his first book, *Palasandra*, and the series of seven new books, *The Kiger Collection*.

The whispers to write came from the horses themselves, saying, "Tell our story so our herd will not be forgotten. We will put our love in your heart." They have done just that. Read more about Mark at Mark's ArtandLemonadeStand.com.

> For I know the plans I have for you declares the Lord. Plans to prosper you and not harm you. Plans to give you hope and a future! (Jeremiah 29:11)

The end. Where it is.